What the Body Remembers

What the Body

Story Line Press
1994

Remembers

poems by Adèle Slaughter

Published by Story Line Press, Inc., Three Oaks Farm, Brownsville,
OR 97327

This publication was made possible thanks in part to the generous
support of the Nicholas Roerich Museum, the Andrew W. Mellon
Foundation, the National Endowment for the Arts, and our individ-
ual contributors.

Text design by Chiquita Babb

Library of Congress Cataloging-in-Publication Data
Slaughter, Adèle.
    What the body remembers : poems / by Adèle Slaughter.
        p.   cm.
    ISBN 0-934257-99-X : $11.95
    I. Title
    PS3569.L269W48   1994
    811'.54—dc20   94-42359
                                          CIP

for Xander

Acknowledgments

I wish to thank the people who encouraged me while I wrote the poems in this book: my family, my teachers, my students. Throughout the years many friends have believed in my poetry and I thank: Frederick Woolverton, who was in on the beginning; Robert McDowell, who knew that this book ought to exist; Dana Gioia whose acute and generous critiques helped to shape many poems in this volume; Stanley Plumly, Sam Toperoff and Stephen Dunn, who helped with the finishing touches. I owe a particular thanks to Hillary Hayes, who not only proofed and proofed the manuscript, but was my support as well. Finally, I am grateful to Robert Olen Butler who gave me so much of what he won.

These poems, sometimes in earlier versions, appeared in the following publications: *The Virginia Quarterly Review*, "The Book of Denial," "Wrestling With My Brother," "Sleeping With My Sisters," and "Piano Lesson." *Long Island Quarterly*: "Snow White Waking" and "Keeper of Childhood"; *Brookspring 89*: "Pregnant With You"; *Confrontation*: "Poem To Save A Marriage"; *Dryad*: "A Tree To Climb"; *NEBO*: "The End of Summer"; *Princeton Spectrum*: "Blossom"; *The Reaper*: "Sestina: Sunday Dinner"; *Waves*: "The Waves."

The series of three sonnets titled "The End Of Summer" was also printed in a limited-edition chapbook by *Aegis Press* at West Chester University.

"Animal Tamer's Wife" first appeared in the anthology *The Poet's Job: To Go Too Far*.

"Snow White Waking" also appeared in the Doubleday Book & Music Club anthology, *Masterpieces of Terror and the Unknown*, edited by Marvin Kaye.

Contents

I

II

III

I

Every creative artist produces a world of his own. Even when he believes himself to be a complete realist and sets himself the task of faithfully reproducing the external world, he, in fact, only uses elements of the existing external world to create with them a reality of his own. According to Proust, an artist is compelled to create by his need to recover his lost past.

—from *A Psycho-Analytical Approach To Aesthetics* by Hanna Segal

A Child's Friend

You filled the pocket of my
green woolen shorts.
My knees knocked like
a furious woodpecker.
Even the Shetland wool blanket
I knit the summer before
could not warm away this knocking.

But you, stone fish, friend,
you could ease me. I recall how
the damp Scottish weather and the
immense green stretched out for days.
I counted the minutes first, then
hours, until finally
dawn and dusk.

Stone fish of abalone,
you fit smooth in my hands.
My sweat was your ocean.
Comfort was to rub you,
wish on your elongated body,
pointing your nose toward home.
Alone in my room, on dark nights,

I set you in a circle with other friends:
Blue stone, tiger's marble, silver scissors,
spool of thread, needle.
This was my own Stonehenge.
Here is where I charted
my way back and I am still
traveling toward home.

A Tree To Climb

Climbing, I
grasp a leaning branch;
the rough surface rips my hand.
I leave white skin under bark.
Under fingernails
tree skin climbs with me.

Limbs hold me in black skies.
Yellow specked pears and I
sit and wait
the only sound is
my breath, short gasps.
The pears won't even breathe.

The bathroom light slices the dark.
A limb grabs my hair
as I jump from the tree.
I take a yellow pear.
In the dark I sneak
to avoid knifing light.

I peek through the window—
my father stands clutching
a pair of silver scissors
cutting Margaret's hair.
I want to scream from my belly.

Instead, I cut my teeth into the pear
run back to the tree
and finish the last slivers.

Keeper of Childhood

Shadows gently fall on ricepaper screens.
        Goldfishes' tails flicker: orange feathers.
Hideko san, we swept into your small life.
        You held our hands to cross Tokyo's streets.

You watched over us; stick legs playing
        kick-the-can in back alleys.
Every Saturday night you asked Mother:
        "Can I go to bath now?" Left us

with sweet rice cakes wrapped in seaweed.
        Your kimono fluttered between your legs
like butterfly wings. Your shuffle like a whisper.
        In the bathhouse: pearl-necks nibbled by shadow.

At our house a spider spins its front gate.
        Tears of confetti rained on you at the dock.
Hideko san, keeper of my childhood—you are
        like mist over lake, shadow of goldfish.

Blossom

A Chickadee repeats its name.
Poplar leaves flip over to white,
keeping time to the wind.
Wrens urge six young from the nest.
My aunt says, "Busy as a wren
is something our family understands."

All summer we waited and now
watch the night-blooming cereus
press open white petals.
I imagine novices, fingers
busy with the rosary,
threading souls with white beads,
fragrance fills the stair landing.
The bloom lasts one night.

I remember kneeling down,
my mother settled into an easy chair,
pulling my head onto her lap
to check my ears for wax.
I have loved the wrong thing.

Hortense: Of the Garden

We were of an age and in an age
when large girls did not burn,
but hid in thin cupboards under uniforms.
"Miss, please sit quietly,
and be careful not to soil your white gloves."

In the auditorium we squirmed
chairs, smiles, clapping
awkward, bruised shines, boney knees.
Playground—we blazed blindly and chewed
a wet, sweet wad of bubble gum,
dirt under our fingernails,
knees skinned and scabbed.
We fingered, read and traded
Nancy Drew mysteries.

Larks in the green countryside,
spun out on a playground full of pears
our cheeks like red currents.
Two big girls, Hortense and me.
A heaven of woods,
something to marvel,
in our school girl uniforms,
with starched collars turned round.
We were a pair of herons
crossing the borders of the kept, Catholic gardens,
leaving the chapels and songbirds behind.

The Book Of Denial

Nothing has ever happened.
This is the dark place at which we begin and end.
Questions only smear the ink, stop
the presses, undo silence with words.

Obvious words stand out, rubbing their sounds together.
Questions throw open the window
letting in light and a stray sparrow.
A bird flies at your face with its pointy beak.

A scared sparrow tries to escape.
You throw a blanket over your head,
open the window and hope for the best.
The questions fly away, look back at the story.

The bird was never really here.
In fact we aren't here either and both of us
are too polite to mention Father,
who inhales several thick martinis with olives.

And we do not sit in a dining room
darkening at sunset, eating bouillabaisse.
He does not smear half a stick of butter on bread, or slump
into his soup. His food doesn't make a ring around the bowl.

To keep all this from happening
we think each other's thoughts,
read each other's minds, finish each other's sentences
and lick each other's plates.

We read our book alone in the dark before bed.
With blankets pulled over our heads,
a family that sticks together can safely say:
nothing has ever happened.

A Sestina: Sunday Dinner

By the old Claud Tom's house hollyhocks open,
an Irish setter yelps, splits the quiet
morning. Mother fills our house with the smell
of waffles, cinnamon and maple syrup. Flavors
wake me, my mouth waters. I feel a touch
of past mornings and wonder if what I know

can be recovered. Will I ever be able to know
that again? Will ripe pears be cut open
on the bread-board? Down the backstairs I touch
the handstained walls. The kitchen's quiet,
Father gone, Mother gardening. Bacon's flavors
rush against my face. I brew coffee, the smell

brings Mother in for another cup, an earth smell
on her clothes and hands. We both know
I don't belong, I'm taller, the flavor's
different. I search for a spoon and open
the towel drawer. She chatters, I keep quiet
and can't picture the faces, trying to touch

what I almost remember, nothing to touch.
Fruit flies circle the smell
of ripe peaches. Her stories tire me, quiet
stretches between us. She doesn't know
what to say, asks if I've decided what flavor
Jell-o I want for dessert. I say, there's open

ice cream and recall hating how Jell-o in open
air forms a slick skin hard to the touch.
I have her mouth, wide face, and also like the flavor
of vanilla best. Out back, the trash burns, I smell
the Spring onions and tomatoes and know
every hidden rock, tree and stream: quiet

places away from the family where the quiet
of people together deafens me. I open
the screen door to escape to a place they don't know.
At dusk, I stare at the blue sky, touch
my knees with my nose and inhale my own smell.
Smoke darkens the sky, smoke and childhood flavors.

A chicken bastes, the flavor bakes in our quiet
house, the smell of Sunday dinner. I know
each time we open our lives we reach and cannot touch.

A Secret Truth

for M. L. K.

What is
the secret ingredient
of a tiny fist
clutching, pounding against
his Aunt Bertha's breast?
The secret
lies deep in the dark of
the tiny fist—a fist
like the spiny skeleton of a starfish
turned into itself.
Dark, dark, dark fist
strikes Aunt Bertha's chest,
stars of light cry out
from her mouth.
When she couldn't be trusted
his life began.
It is a sad truth that
the beginning of life
is the beginning of mistrust.
Each of us is born on a planet
where rain never falls
and when we feel our first drop
of rain, we're here.
There has to be some explanation.
Why did the little boy
with his tiny fist
look at Aunt Bertha that way?
Because it begins and ends this way.
On this planet with
the tiny fist, Bertha's breast,
falling rain and our mistrust
of anything abstract
we can see
many billions of years away
a star dying.

Wrestling With My Brother

Michael, given the name of an archangel,
the son our parents could not have,
you shared your adopted life with me.
In Grandma's Virginia we rode horses reckless,
bareback, through the fields like hounds,
calling to the early moon.
After dark, we climbed a pear tree
to reach through the night, hug the moon.
On cold ground around a fire you built,
you captured me with confusing stories
of mice with wings flying into everything.
You convinced me the owl used
our marbles for his eyes.
Before I grew breasts, you wrestled me
to the ground; held me down as my face grew hot.
You taught me how to do the twist
to Chubby Checkers howling "shake it up, baby."
I was all your little sis and planned
to marry you when I grew up.

But they never believed you—
you said you saw a fly sitting on the nose of the deer in the far field.
Father could not stop beating you into truth.
After the night he took you out to the shed
and cracked a board against your backside
like a dog he'd break in,
you stuck out your thumb,
made it to Florida. All those people,
and you picked up for vagrancy.
No glory left, you joined the Army.
Nights, I shiver in our pear tree and call to you:
Lost brother, lost brother, lost.

My Father's Hands

ran through his army crew-cut,
a hairbrush bristling on his head,
he was a smile that could win a horserace,
he'd arrive we'd shout, "Daddy's home."
We stood at attention,
he measured our growth,
taught us how to make a bed,
pull the corners taut,
his big hands deft, sandpaper fingers skipped
a quarter off the blanket. No ripples.

Every two years we moved: Army Gypsies.
Memories live in particular houses,
in cities where my father was stationed.
On Willamore Way, in Baltimore
he hugged me, I lost my breath,
pointed toward a pile of toys. Daddy, let me go.
Daddy stopped a lawn mower from chopping my sister down,
as if he could hold the blades, cut a piece of finger off.
In Yellow Springs, Maryland
he chased me through our honeysuckled house.
On the stair landing he caught me, those big hands
tickled me till I cried. Daddy, let me go.

In Tokyo we flew two cloth fish in the wind.
One for Papa San, a smaller for Brother San.
Proudly we displayed the men of our household:
a Japanese tradition. In our quiet house that
bordered the alley, the whisperings of women
lay like light fluttering through rice-paper screens,
like goldfish reflecting orange in a dark pool.

Father threw a tea cup at Brother San's face,
slashed open the rice-paper window, breaking

the light that fell on the walls of our house.
Father was angry his eyes swirled red like bourbon.
He clenched his jaw and called my name.
Daddy, let me go.
I tried to swim into the deep corners of the dark pool,
Daddy, let me go.
But his huge hands slowly undid his belt buckle.
He covered my bottom with butterfly bruises.
I blamed myself for crying.
Daddy, let me go.

His final move back to the States was to farm country.
He grows roses, drinks gin, counts fireflies;
and late at night, trips, dead drunk, over croquet hoops.
His stomach swollen like a bloated, river rat.
His red-rimmed eyes brittle like china cups,
filled with the blackest tea, hidden leaves, fortuneless.
At dinner, he blows his nose into
the palm of his practical hands,
big hands that built a yellow doll house for me.
The same hands I now have.
Daddy, let me go.

American Summer

1. Portents

Hot attic. Dead flies, bees in corners, on the windowsill.
A thick swarm of broken insects, burnt, brittle.
Stacks of saved newspapers smell burnt like
a hot iron scorching cloth.

Barefoot among the bees we open the army-green trunk,
pull out party dresses. Blood-red silk, full skirt,
a crinoline petticoat of horsehair and linen.
Imagine, a skirt and petticoat and mother's long legs.

An attic parade. A star spangled string of kids
in oversized clothes. The red dress like an amaryllis.
An American flag draped, like the copper gown of the Statue of Liberty.
A Chaplin hat on a girl in a pink tutu wearing a man's jacket.

Dogs in from a run, hot, wet and thick with dog smell.
Brother and I inspect the red hair for ticks,
happy to find gray bodies fat with blood. Carefully,
we pull off the ticks, heads intact, burn them on the sidewalk.

The parade ends at the bottom of the attic stairs.
We wash the dogs in tomato juice to rid them of skunk smell
the ticks burnt, we sweep up the dead insects.
All around is summer and signs of the end.

2. Vehicles

Every other year Father bought a Ford, traded in
the one he drove the long commute to D.C.
cleaning his car I found those little bottles of gin, or whiskey

bottles that kept straight like soldiers, empty under his car seat.
He always bought Fords. We were an American family.

Memorial day the family piled in our stationwagon and drove
to Grandfather's grave, with peonies.
Afternoon back at the cold, stone house Grandmother
sipped her bourbon, drank and drank until liquor
and cough medicine dripped off her blue hair.

We were an American family, playing into dusk—
us kids hid in boxwood, breathing in the green, earth smell
that smell never left our skin, filled our nostrils.
Our parents sat on the stone porch,
the smell of bourbon seeped into their bodies.

3. *In The Hollow Of The Hand*

She let Grandfather's grape vines go.
Each summer we got fewer and fewer Concord grapes.
Perfectly round, dark-purple spheres,
sweet and sour all mixed together,
Grapes I gathered into the hollow of my hand,
peeled them with my teeth,
held the tender membrane in my mouth,
savoring the taste the way Dad and Grandma savored
the cocktail hour until they were
immersed in bourbon mashed with bitters and sugar.
I picked and ate grapes off the vine,
and gathered the seeds with lips, tongue and teeth,
trying to separate the thick mucus from seed.

4. Equestrian

She rides the biggest horse, the one they call "Boy."
He wants to run and run—so the girl lets him go
until his sweat and heavy breathing scare her.
Squeezes her legs tight, the reins taut.
"Come on 'Boy' let's go back."
He rears, his white head back, up on hind legs.
The girl presses the length of her body against his.
They descend to the ground,
he lands on four feet. Up again,
again they come down together.
The third time she leans, they land on their backs.
The saddle cracks as "Boy" rolls off her.
The girl limps out of the paddock, lies down on the grass.
What is the father now, who watched the whole scene,
what is he to do? It is simple to him.
He throws one leg up over, in hand, firmly,
the horse disappears over the ridge walking sure-footed,
unable to gallop under her father's hand.

How is the girl now, who has lost her ride.
How is she, alone on the grass
as her father clicks his tongue,
guides it back up the hill into the next field.
She realizes her first lesson
in a world of men and women. She will be thrown—
She will not always stay on.

And underneath the fear and anger in my heart
I learned the pleasure of the moment
and how to get up afterwards, even with a sprained knee,
how to stand up and walk.

II

Fortunately, psychoanalysis is not the only way to resolve inner conflicts. Life itself remains a very effective therapy.

—from *Our Inner Conflicts* by Karen Horney

Desire

The sweet laundry smell, in winter.
The touch of the sun's smooth
yellow fingers: reached through the glass door
into the lingering afternoon
and laid hot fingers across our young necks.
We were on the look out for intruders
hidden under a table
piled high with loaves of laundry,
here we spied on the world.
Bobby and me all knees and elbows dirty.
We giggled, whispered through my autumn hair
our cheeks red from the cold, white snow all around.

Here, I was within the grasp of my first
boy who wanted to explore
the dark night of my mouth.
Thin arms circled waists, our chests met.
Child-breasts; sparks igniting star points.
As we tossed and fumbled,
sheets and towels tumbled:
a fallen tower of Mother's work.
Our laundry nest scattered about the porch.
Afraid, I stopped—but the wanting
buzzed in my ears and with the young boy
and the icicles melting off the side of the house
I felt something stirring in my gut,
rising to my throat, like a leopard waiting to leap.
Was this what they meant?

1970

In the back seat of a friend's Buick
lined in chrome, seats in black leather,
Dave Kelly's nails are bitten,
and his hands are all over my thighs.
For the first time
it doesn't feel right or wrong.
It's just kissing and kissing
Dave Kelly from New Brunswick.

Summer afternoon—I wait on the mailman.
Dave's time at 4-H camp seems to stretch
like the flavor of bubble-gum never does.
Penciled letters in a bitten scrawl
keep my thighs hot, sticking to black leather
and me masturbating in the bathroom.

Another basketball season,
we talk on the phone
he's so far away and all I can think
of is him and me in the back seat,
but he's talking about Mary,
how fine and sweet she is, how he likes her.
Mary with redder hair than mine,
Mary younger than me.
Mary my sister.
One of my four sisters.
And at my scream
old Dave Kelly hangs up the phone
and I'll never see him again,
but neither will Mary.

Piano Lesson

On the edge of town
in a brick house that stood
next to the white stucco church on the corner
lived the preacher and my piano teacher.
Standing out front I imagined the smell of the
inside; oak paneling like cinnamon
and the piano that sat
like a librarian facing the front door.

The door opened to an empty house.
Waiting for her I played
the one piece I could play.
At the recital in the white stucco church,
everyone cried when I played "Love is Blue."
The keys clicked under my hands
and the music moved through my body and out my palms.

The sun set and still no one came.
I wandered through the house.
At their bedroom I stopped.
Looking at the king size bed,
the rumpled sheets,
I thought of her. She was full bottomed but
thin up top. Her hair and hands fluttered.
The preacher was thick like a potato.
Sometimes he appeared during my lesson,
his pockets ringing: potato fists of loose change—
his children scrambled to the floor for what he discarded.

I stared into the preacher's open closet:
belts hanging on a nail, dirty socks trailing
into the room. Behind a row of ties I saw a box
the size of a dishwasher. I peeked inside.

It was filled with *Playboys*.
The preacher's secret congregation called to me
to become a member. I stared
at the red tipped nipples of the round breasts,
at the wet lips and tongue tips.
I felt my thirteen years press against my flat chest.

I thought, "Get out of this closet, practice."
She'd listen and sigh at a phrase well done.
She said, "With your large hands you can reach
more than an octave. You have such a good ear.
More practice," she begged.
But instead I shared the preacher's secret calling
and hid in our warm attic
drawing pictures of naked women
rubbing my thighs together.

Sleeping With My Sisters

1

Nights we all piled into the same double bed.
A huddled mass of elbows and rear ends.
Each massaging, scratching, begging
another to rub her back.
The little two got crammed in between
our arm pits, honeysuckle on the vine.
Five, and I was the biggest,
the one that took everything first—
even stepped on a rusty nail
saving my sisters the shot, the infection.

2

Mary fought me—
a sister with more hip and bigger breasts.
She was choppy: cut-red curls, stormy eyes.
Her nails bitten, no moon showing.

Contrary, a curl, so proud of being so very good
and so very bad.
Sister—dark and wild.
Her hips are wide and spread easily
but tight like a wet wish bone
she opens to let men in.
They only get one wish.

She was like humid weather
I learned to endure.
Her temper sat in a cold bucket
turning her white skin red.

When her lower lip shoved out
the others gave her anything she wanted
to keep her calm,
but not from me.

3

Fighting was a kind of loving.
That Sunday all us girls were crammed in the back seat—
I got the window—
She pinched my thigh.
After church, I took the bottom sheet off her bed.
She ripped the bedding off mine
leaving a bare mattress and a bed to make.
I threw hers down the stairs.
A rage of hot wind flew at me.
I turned. My fist landed in the middle of her back.
Winded she slumped.
Her fingertips scratched the wooden floor.

4

It is night life now. He rises above me
looking like a man on a cross,
his hands supporting himself over my body.
His right leg tucked behind his left,
he is pushing himself into me,
searching for a sweet spot.
I press my legs into the small of his back.
Just as I climb up toward his breath,
I miss sleeping with those sisters—

I miss the honeysuckle—the sweet smell fills my lungs.
They are in my skin, rubbing my back,
tangled in the sheets. Please, little sister
rub my back just a little longer.

Poem For The Voyeur

You are hidden.
Look in the window,
a family gathers
around the dinner table.
The father breathes in a gin martini.
Perhaps it is his third in the last hour.
No one is counting and you just got here.

Look at the child, she's ten,
pale and covered with freckles.
You want to see inside her heart?
Open her chest, like a stuffed doll's
it can be sewn up.
You can even put a zipper down her front
for your pleasure.

Tonight she is setting the table
concentrating on matching the silverware.
You notice the daughter's movements are jerky.
Listen to her think:
He might hit me or want to hold me on his lap
and rub against my legs.
She is excited, thinking of being on his lap.
She wants to run away from this feeling
like a horse galloping, but the reins are
held in, her eyes are pulled behind her head.

Tonight, you watch him eat with his hands,
glob butter on his roll,
a ring of food stains the tablecloth
in the shape of his plate.
Finally he belches and passes out.
The weight of his stomach holds him up,

his head rests on his chest.
Relief is in her heart and
blooms like a poppy, thin, fragile and orange.

Look again, he's waking up
breathing heavily. She wrinkles her nose
at the smell of gin.
He pulls off his belt, looking her over,
shouts "Come here you!" Sweat drips down her back.
With each lick the leather burns, her tears
come faster until her whole face is wet.
Look at his crotch, his penis is hard.

She planned not to submit to this,
to be stiff like her plastic Barbie doll,
but when the welts swell on the small of her back
she lets go, cries and urinates in a pool at her feet.
In the hall mirror she watches tears roll down her face.
Go ahead, unzip her heart.
Red welts circle around her crotch.
Soon no one will penetrate her
and only voyeurs, like you, will look
into her little heart.

Boy at Dawn

He twists under the feather quilt
and reaches between the sheets, but comes
up empty. Blue coal shadows slash
her white skin, her eyes are
cups of black tea. She says —

       I dreamed of wings flapping,
calling my name over and over.
The thin bones and skin
fossilized.

He wants to lay his hands on her hair
and take a kiss, an apple-seed, a star,
a pinpoint of light on water.
He doesn't. The sun rises, stars recede,
orange is the morning sky.

She pulls her swimsuit over her
blue breasts and ties back
her hair. By the time she leaves
he is dreaming of a phantom girl
swimming out into the black river.

O

On the Long Island Railroad
to New York City
the businessman sitting next to me
wears the musky cologne you wore.
The heavy smell of it brings
the full force of my memory of you.
I hear your voice, the slow deliberate vowels
that circled your words and were round
like your mouth, always in an 'o',
like oh, that is what you want?

I see your thick fingers wrap a bottle of Heineken
and you put the indifferent glass 'o' up to your
wet, oh, that is what you want.
All the while your moaning eyes stare at me.
A deep shadow darkens your cheeks.
My sex swells up toward you.
You suck in your upper lip.
Oh, I know what I want,
and won't take it.
I will smell you, glide my thighs past your eyes,
all rising, swelling and never, never
did I take it all.
Yet some ten years later
I am naked riding this train,
you circle my clitoris
and oh, I remember you, my stranger.

Assigning Jealousy

Women make me bleed
or at the very least blood
pounds at my fingertips, temples, toes.
Like this model-perfect blond
that works at the hospital where I work:
all frosted curls and cold blue eyes,
those eyelashes and small feet and hands.
As if she doesn't menstruate
or sit down real fast
on the edge of a cold porcelain bowl
after some guy left the seat up.
Every time she walks by me,
I take in her fingernails and clothes;
yesterday she had on beige pants
and a silk shirt with delicate bamboo.
I saw her from a distance on the street.
For the first time I noticed how short she is.
She twisted her ankle ever so slightly
on cracked pavement, just the way I do.

I even had a dream about her:
all I remember is
I wanted to spit on her face
and kiss her face all at the same time.
Since she got into my dreams,
guess I have to come to terms with her.
I'm sure I'm the only woman who feels like this—
hating and loving other women.
Look at me, look at me.
I'm talking about a cold, beautiful woman
and you are looking at me.

Skinned Alive

Everyday some small betrayal
eats a piece of my mask.

Unrestrained by the strict rules of verse
a word spoken, "thigh," "caress,"
or some tenderness leads me to a corner—
there lies the betrayal and the betrayed.

The blush, the most infamous apostate.
Once mastered—the art of the blush—
works to my advantage as in chicanery,
hiding that uses honesty as a cover.

There is the betrayal of a friend.
To get close to you
I disclose a small, but essential secret truth,
behind her back. This entails guts—

Impaled by the betrayal, nailed down.
I am splayed open—
on the dissecting table; my body split in two;
my mask peeled. Skinned alive.

My liver: small, hard, and red
oozing mustard of intestines,
resembling those dozen or so hard-shelled
crabs I've scooped and scooped;

and spit out the bitter guts on brown paper
for the waitress and janitor to clean.

Snow White Waking

Slam your fist through the glass coffin.
I have been lying here for so long,
my body dark, my mind blank.
I have forgotten touch.
Does red lick milk from a bowl,
does black caw or is that the night?
What's that buzz in my ears—
ice thawing or a fly?

I am so relieved you are here
but cannot speak or move.
You reach between the sheets.
My hands clutch an apple to my breast.
That witch meant it to be forever,
but you are here and it is not forever.
Come hold me. My arms are stiff,
Has frost bit my fingers?
A weak pulse throbs through my body.

Black is the hair on my head and curls
between my legs. Hair, black like
night next to the day of my white skin.
Come hold both the day and the night.
The flies, dogs, cats and parakeets
are buzzing back to life and yes
the ice is melting. I can almost feel you.
Come closer, breathe your milk-breath on my face.
Red is a color, red is blood and rushes to my lips
and flows from my legs. Come kiss me.

Catherine

walks through corridors to class
the sound of wooden rosary beads,
the rustle of skirts. A silver cross
pinned to her chest
reflects in the eyes of her girls.
The smell of bread mold and wet attics
is her perfume. Sister Catherine stuck her
finger with a needle sewing relics into blessed cloth.
Bones in linen and a small red stain under the altar.

Catherine, with a handkerchief up her sleeve,
has fingers pricked red as her nose. Allergies she says.
Her face: pink, young, blue eyes,
clear as if she just finished crying.
Dusk, black robed women, a long pine table,
clay bowls full of bean soup. They do not speak
while they eat. Catherine rips apart the bread she kneaded
that afternoon, dunks it in black soup.

Night, cloistered nuns in a dorm room.
Sister Claire pulls a brush with horsehair bristles
through Catherine's red hair, electric, flying in the air
like ten thousand hands reaching out.
Rows of beds. Women in white nightgowns.
White cotton against pale skin.
Skin finally breathing.
Catherine slips from the sheets.
Her red hair falls long, gentle on her shoulders.

She does not put on her slippers
to take her moonlit stroll, nor does she walk on a path.
Instead her feet sink in wet grass—
dirt between her toes—she lifts up her nightgown

and walks beside boxwood bushes that scratch her legs.
Catherine leans against a cold stone wall
breathing in the starry air. Wind lingers
between her thighs. She picks a slug off the brick walk—
it lays a wet, thick stream on the palm of her hand.

Joan

Slender girl steps out of her armor
metal breast-plate blackened by mud
slung up from horses' hooves.

Her neck: a soft curve.
Hands, legs, buttery skin,
cropped bangs: golden-brown flowers
embroidered on her skull.

Birds fly out when she opens her hands,
her tongue fills the air with prophecies,
her thighs are sweet honeysuckle,
flowers to eat, mouths shaped like sugar cones
drink in the juice of honey rain.

Lightly, on hot embers
she walks through the war camp.
Her men follow her,
smell her every move.

She bursts into flames,
the air heavy with the burning of buttery flesh.
Joan, cauterized by irons on her feet and hands,
hissing, sizzling she stands
eyes turned up to the sky.

Dead Women Poets

the ones not afraid to die:
went out in a gaseous cloud, an oven;
swallowed pills,
consumed in an alcoholic haze.
Dead women poets,
the ones not afraid to die
are buried in Daddy's shroud.
Lie next to him in the ground,
heads tucked in his arm pit,
married to his brutal hands.

Dead women poets are not like us.
We are survivors, wheeling in a chair,
walking with canes and crutches,
wrapped in gauze hiding scars and stitches.
Flesh and bone grind away our synovia,
saliva drying up, mouths parched.
We limp on our tendons
tight in the mornings, out of bed
moving to the bathroom,
our bladders nearly burst.

Survivors sing the blues
and risk it all just to feel alive.
Our pockets, too full of stones
for us to be balloons or butterflies.
Dead women poets whisper
across our faces like eyelashes;
breathe on us in our sleep.
When we wake we wear their pain
as if it is our own.

Dead women poets congregate;
dead women poets, who showed their bare arms,
lifted up their skirts and enjoyed doing so.
Dead women poets gather round our poems
urge us to do more than just survive,
do more than touch and smell.
Urge us not to die until
our last breath swallows itself, and we're turned into
dead women poets: the ones who lived.

Anatomy

Close to the bone, ankle bone, shin bone,
knee bone is soft muscle and ligament.
Under skin, fingerprint and nail is bone.
Wrist, vein, nerves wrapped around bone.
Soft pulse of blood, throbs, throbs.

And the shoulders, a gentle curve; a place for
lips and tongue to rest in the dip of clavicle
joined to the breast bone. Close to the bone, lies the heart.
Soft, beating blue blood not touching air.

Under rib bones lies the solar plexus, the interwoven
place where the black hole of self lies breathing,
feeling, love; pain; and all the losses.
A soft sob under the cage of the rib-bone.

Close to the bone, the pelvic bone, between hip bones
is V of bone where he and she press against each other
connecting hair, skin against skin, then nerve, clitoris, cock.
Move closer to bone,
where everything is and is not.

Body Memory

I live for what the body remembers:
cold sheets warmed by the rapid beat of body blood;
the taste of spaghetti, better the next day;
the sight of blue against the furry pines.

Muscles remember the feeling
of getting up on water skis, emerging—water to air—
a baby descending though the body to be born.
Once under hypnosis, images appeared: each muscle
held a scene. Again I saw my fall from a tree,
my father come at me, my brother pull me to my feet.

Suppose the body is compelled to recreate—
Locked in that old fashioned crawl—
repeating and repeating old moves
to keep the body whole, to keep itself from floating
into black space, the limbs separating.

A guitar player moves his hands
across the strings, he picks, pulls, strokes,
urges a new sound out of the body,
and struggles to play a new phrase.
Fingers go back to the known patterns.
Body memory in set rhythms.
Sweat breaks out, jaw clenched.

We strive to recover a lost taste, touch and smell
make it new again, alive again.
Body memory like a finger on the vulva
quelling all thought, the body remembering.
I live for what the body remembers.

III

Do not believe that he who seeks to comfort you lives untroubled
among the simple and quiet words that sometimes do you good.
His life has much difficulty and sadness and remains far behind
yours. Were it otherwise he would never have been able to find
those words.

—from *Letters to a Young Poet* by Rainer Maria Rilke,
translation by M.D. Herter Norton

Looking At The Fat Lady

Eating popcorn, a young man files through the crowd
gaping at rows of side shows: two-headed
babies in formaldehyde, acrobatic dwarfs,
a nymph with a hairy tail, a winged snake,
and the Great Fat Lady. She'd like to change
her name, but recalls her doctor saying,
"Sometimes a cigar is just a cigar."
When she ran away her parents were overjoyed.
Spectators line-up like peas on a knife.

A thin man eaten by pock marks, headed
for the big tent, offers the Lady a toothy grin.
His greased back hair outlines a head like a snake.
He trips and falls. The Lady cackles, she's overjoyed.
The crowd hushes. His eyes are like a knife.
"You laughing at me?" He holds a stick of dynamite,
"Sometimes a cigar," his lip curls, "is just a cigar."
"Come on honey," the Lady lisps and shows her tongue.
He backs off, stepping like a tightrope walker.

A boy clasps his mother's sweaty hand
as she says, "From eating peas on a knife."
The Great Lady has relatives she cannot stand.
A nymphomaniac, arms around her man, in snake
skin heels, tugs at her dress. She'd like to change
but sometimes his cigar is such a cigar.
She wriggles like a mud wrestler. The crowd's
a writhing mass, even bigger than her,
whose sex melts like cotton candy on a tongue.

Identical twins walk round, arm in arm. The Lady
likes to watch the crowd and sees a circle of dwarfs
looking into fun-house mirrors. Although they grin

at their distorted shapes, they'd like to change.
Could she begin to like the relatives she cannot stand?
"Sometimes," she lines up peas to eat off a knife,
she thinks, her hunger keeps her fat and yards apart,
from the hoards of cigars that are just cigars.
When she ran away her parents were overjoyed.

The Animal Tamer's Wife

Stealthy as a shewolf I stalk
the circus camp for mice. Teeth, bones, hair
decompose as slow as disagreements.
The moon spreads my shadow on animal-wet straw.

I was seduced by your rhinestone studded
jacket worn close to your chest.
Your whip kept lions hanging mid-air,
hungry but tame as dogs.

Elephants curled me in their trunks.
You soothed wild cubs with raw beef.
Snakes curled around my toes.
I learned the art of charming.

We stirred the zebras' nostrils, stripes swirled.
You stuffed our mattress with stallion hair
to tame my dreams. Now, nightly, I beat
the camels, panthers, apes. And I prowl.

The Escape Artist

Bound in a straight jacket
a black hood pulled
over his sooty eyes.
His hands are cuffed
behind his back.
The cotton of his tongue
sucks up his cries. He
is always afraid.

His assistant poses in a
red bikini. Her up-tipped
breasts bounce.
Licking wet lips she clicks
her red fingernails against
the glass vat were he is
lowered. Underwater,
inside a trunk, a cocoon,
he is unfolding.
His lungs beat
like butterfly wings.

Butterflies that fill the air
pass on their trembling.
His audience gasps,
their lungs clapping.
The fat lady
forgets her appetite,
the fire-eater
denies his thirst.

The Fortune Teller

I watch her close.
Her body, a whisper
I can barely hear.
She fingers a card
of a woman holding open
the jaws of a lion.

A shudder flutters through her
like bats returning to a cave.
Pressing my palms against
the table, I lean forward,
What is it?

Her head jerks back.
Her eyes flash at me,
full of shooting stars.
Looking away, she scoops up my
spread like a black-jack dealer,
and answers my questions
with empty eyes.

Marriage

1

At the altar in an ivory dress, a crown of cornflowers,
I saw the vision of God the priest had promised:
scenes of my life appeared like dominos—

a lie I hid behind, a fantasy before sleep.
I was meant to forgive myself. It was clear
that I would be confused again and again,

and I could forgive myself that too.
Like the moment of seeing my face
in the bathroom mirror behind the steam,

just wiped away—the vision vanished, steamed over.
The dominos fell, each act touching the next,
linked like pick-up sticks, kissing jacks.

2

In our cottage I walk through the rooms
of our marriage collecting images
like flowers from a cutting garden:

a fly drowsy, still full of winter sleep stirs.
Blue wings against a windowpane. Tiny white,
bell-shaped flowers huddle in the March cold. It was true

we look like brother and sister, and I am afraid
we are two children, not husband and wife—
both of us huddled together in our cottage.

3

Gardens: we plant flowering yellows, whites, purples,
together we try and tame a piece of earth.
Leave the woods beyond the garden wild.

In fall we clean it out, no more leaves.
Rain waters the grass, burnt from the lawnmower.
The yellow, burnt sections revive.

4

There is also comfort, bodies pressed together
in the bedroom of the neat house.
Under the Hudson Bay blanket. Touching.

In the bath you and I sit, hot water steams our thighs red,
stimulates circulation in our bodies. Blood revives.
Marriage has its own body and mind, needs its own revival.

5

When the body is caught up in being practical—earn a living,
drive the kid(s) around, make more money, service the car, more
money, pick up the clock, get curtains made, dry cleaning, bank.

The stuff of a marriage
floats on top of us like cream on milk,
thick—sickening—hard to swallow.

6

Milk-fed veal, a foot nailed to the floor
locked up in a dark room. Lost beauty.
On my hand I twist the wedding band,

a hoop I slip through, an obedient dolphin.
The audience delights at my captive tricks.
The horror of it, a flip of my tail is mistaken

for a friendly wave. Everything I do seen
through the eyes of my trainer who flips me some herring.
Oh, to swim in the darkest reaches of blue.

7

But what is the story here? I hide behind myself
giving you images—dominos, flies,
bell-shaped flowers, milk-fed veal and dolphins.

I become a little i and twist my rings
denying them, a whole life doesn't exist.
Little i wants ten thousand lovers;

The little i buries her left hand deep inside her pocket.
The married i relies on dreaming hands
to hold the way of dreaming.

8

But stories do not end in dreams. We are a myth
misreading each other in crossed and crooked ways.
The aisle was straight, we walked it fighting.

You walk too fast, I walk too slow.
It is all in the timing, our timing is off.
No. Go deeper, dig into the flesh, two flesh can be as one.

Flip a coin, heads we merge, tails we stay apart.
It lands standing up. The marriage gods
laugh. Light and shadow intermingle.

Poem To Save A Marriage

Please notice
the delicate
blue, three-petal flowers
on the windowsill

and also
that I've washed
our dinner dishes
from last night.

Pregnant With You

there's a pond between my legs.
My belly full of fat fish,
fish tails flip and hit at my sides.

I dreamt I heard
a scream inside me.
I had to cut you out.
Blood on my hands.
You came out
an infant with my father's face.
Your blue skin stretched tight.

I shift to my right side
to move you off my sciatic nerve
where you lie, numbing my legs.
I rub my warm, hard belly
and roll onto my stomach
to sleep, undisturbed,
but your head presses against my diaphragm.
Breathless, I think of how
I might smother you
the way my father squeeze-hugged me
just to say hello: I'm home.

You stir inside me.
Your legs, arms and elbows
poking at me, pulling
at the roots of my past.
Will I need you too much?

Closing my eyes I look inside
my body. Between my breasts glows
light, filtering through yellowed maple leaves.

I look at you: bright, luminous, fearless,
an incandescent filament.
You are new to me.
My light looks yellow and sad next to yours.

The Waves

split
and crack up on the beach
reaching my toes.
Salt water, sticky like pickle brine,

rises
then falls: a heart beat
rubbing down my thighs.
The undertow unevenly tugs

sand;
the ocean floor pulls back
the floor beneath my feet.
Hazy foam

obscures
the horizon, gray-green.
I lose you in sea space and
comb your water nest,

searching
whitecaps, cloud-like
for your crow-black head.
The water is choppy. I

find
you unaware, deep in play, shimmering
as I often notice light does on top
of water. My

gaze
like a lighthouse beam
sweeps gently over surfaces
unconscious of undercurrents or

riptides
that might suck you out
away from my line of vision. I
cannot prevent each and every

accident
so I struggle to be content
with watching, which gives you, or is it me
company.

Renaming Depression

And the Eskimos
with twenty six words for snow,
Such a fine alertness
to what variously presses down.
—Stephen Dunn

Call it Despair—sleepless nights—
waking at four a.m. The mind racing to the next
chore, and the next until they screech and peel out
leaving rubber on the pavement.
Call it Heartache, the emptiness inside the barrel
of the body, the well where no coins drop.
Where hellos come back disembodied.
Call it Melancholia, a low spirited self
lifts up like heavy drapes full of dust, you wheeze and weep.
Call it Despondency, a Teddy bear stuck with a pin.
It does not respond. The Teddy always grins—
until you find it lifeless, stuffing strewn across the nursery floor.

Don't call it moody or mumpish
although you are swollen and out of shape.
It is not sorrow or grief because no one has died,
not anyone we can give a funeral to or actually bury.
You are not morose or somber because those words imply
something happened to cause you pain.
This feeling of hopelessness now exists in spite of your mother.
You are eating out your heart. To your horror,
you find yourself with trembling hands
and cannot eat real food—just the stored up food of self.
You are listless all Sunday long, the worst day
for its lack of structure. Soul-sick,
everything and nothing you can say preys on your mind.

You are sullen, gloomy, in the dumps
and not really very good company.
Even though I poke fun for relief,

it hurts when I manage to understand such despair.
I am disheartened by your desolate soul.
I would put my hands in front of the nails,
but like Mary I have to watch this pain
until you come back to life, and learn once more
love, light, wind, fire, and the pleasure
of earth when plants grow and move the dirt aside.

Domestic Landscape, Dream Landscape

A revolving door circles under the streets
spitting out a stream of people. We start
the long climb to Bloomingdales.
New sheets redefine our bed.
We return dripping with red clay from dreams
deep in the core, the earth's center.
Come back to a dent in the blue station wagon,
come back to start the lawnmower, to rake leaves,
to sweep the white kitchen floor,
pile up wood, fluff pillows, glue a broken toy,
mend stockings.

I was running through a tunnel,
scaling down a mountain,
the lead rope tight on my waist,
swimming up, up from darkness,
toward light, toward air, toward warmth,
to a solid wall, thick.
I tried to break through—
you pressed your whole body against it,
burned your way through.
And here among the cut flowers, dried leaves,
among the dogwoods, Hawthorn tree,
drinking herb tea, and me off coffee,
here, we are dormant bulbs in the new garden.
Here we live with shadows and winter coming.
On long dark nights we remember
to take out the garbage.

I must learn to live alone. Learn
clock and self. Not self through other,
self through self. Hide all the mirrors in the house.
Sweep the dust balls from under the bed,

throw the television into the closet.
Sit with my shoes and listen to their sad stories.
I must find the place in the wall you burned.
Inner world of hot clay, corridors filled
with terror. Solitude possesses me.
Yet I try to throw my aloneness on you
the way light filters though a screen and the pattern
looks familiar, like the shape of my face in a mirror.

Boiling Pantoum

When I cook, I boil you.
Your breath fills the room,
steams the windows. I cry
from dicing onions.

Your breath fills the room.
I knead you into little rolls.
While dicing onions
I cried. I would do anything for you.

I need you. Make little rolls
full of butter. Are you too rich
I cried? I would do anything for you,
sauté a forest of mushrooms

filled with butter, it's all too rich
but let's eat it anyway while
sautéing a forest of mushrooms.
I'll put you on a bed of lettuce.

Let's eat anyway while
wrapping your soul with black caviar.
I'll put you on a bed of lettuce,
careful not to boil the water away.

I wrap sole with black caviar,
set the table, light candles
careful not to boil the water away.
When I cook for you, steam is on the windows.

The End Of Summer

I The Corn Puppet

August was a love-making bed, a long caress.
Twisted sheets of rain laid down the wheat.
Now the days shorten and lengthen my sadness.
Cold sweeps in from the North behind the heat.

The leaves were fireworks in September air.
Red, yellow, brown, they fade into dark.
And I am buried underground to where
Death stole Persephone. This life is stark.

Like a leafless tree I mirror my destruction,
A corn puppet sewn into a winter coat.
Faithful, childless, rotting, I am no one.
The food of the dead sticks in my throat.

Now in my grave of frozen earth
No voices will enchant me back to birth.

II The Queen Persephone

The sun sinks, sapped of its great heat.
Sleep is an unbroken poppy field, scarlet
Faces with lazy grins. And dying I repeat
The weather. Arguments that held my heart

Fall, withered by the frost. Riddles remain
Hanging like bats curled under eaves.
I puzzle out my choices, and return to the same
Celibate place. Now I grow ill at ease.

And yet my desolation is premature,
Just as death is a shock even after illness.
We have this in common: need for pure
Tears, rage and desire for the kiss.

Can I make a stubborn peace with life
That lacks the sharp seduction of a knife?

III Demeter

Walking over this bleak ground, laid bare
As my life, I recall the spring earth.
Rich plowed fields, lusty as a pear
Ripe in my hands. Now, stubble breaks forth.

The short-eared owl filled this past November
With the noisy story of the light we lost
And of my daughter, gone, who took with her
My voice, my face, my heart. I am a ghost

Of myself. All I want or need is absent,
With no husband for comfort or for pleasure.
I burn the gathered leaves—my last dissent.
The fire flares. Warming my hands, I wonder:

How will I repeat my life, all this again
Embodied only in my daughter's skin?

After September

Autumn harvest, fall of the leaf, all hallow summer.
Pumpkin, jack-o-lantern, watchman at my door.
Jack's night-light flickers, plays with the dark.
Crooked stick clothed in rags, Scarecrow—
scares even the wind, such weird sisters screech,
run through gardens and fields of rotting acorn squash,
cucumbers, eggplants, mad apple, peppers, beets
scarlet runners wrap their voodoo, hoodoo vines
around our vespers. Sing an evening song, enchant
the ghosts I lay down on my shedding self.
Smoke rises from the ground and out of my mouth.
Chilled air. Soon all the parsley, chives, nasturtium
lavender and thyme will be charmed by the frost
and my body too, slowed by Autumn's spell.

Yes

We are free to choose our children's
arms, a man or woman's embrace.
With choice your breath is not stale to me
but sweet: the smell of sex.
Undress and you are beautiful,
the bed sheets twist full of our smells,
and you do not block the doorway.

I do not feel fettered here.
I can come and I can go—
each day I stay, I stay.
Out of my head flow colored threads,
from every pore they thread and
weave into your eyes.

Yes, I am sewn into your fabric.
Let me hug and kiss you.
Your lips cover mine. Firm.
Your tongue thrusting into my mouth.
Will you settle back just a little?
I'll teach you where to touch
my undulant white skin,
you can reach inside my breast bone,
there is no place I won't let you go.
I am finished holding back.

Notes on the Poems

Looking At The Fat Lady

This poem is in the form of a "fugue." The fugue is a form originally suggested in a poem by Weldon Kees. Dana Gioia designed the fugue form in a poem titled "Lives of the Great Composers." Howard Moss wrote two more poems in the fugue form, both titled "More Lives of the Great Composers."

The fugue form is four, nine line stanzas. After the first stanza, in the successive three stanzas, a number of phrases are repeated. Which phrases are repeated, the order of the phrases repeated and how many times a given phrase is repeated is random.

© 1993 DAVID RAMAGE

About the Author

ADÈLE SLAUGHTER earned an M.F.A. from Columbia University. She has worked as a teacher to recovering addicts, homeless people, high school dropouts, and hospital patients. In 1993 she was honored by the White House Commission on Presidential Scholars as a Distinguished Teacher.